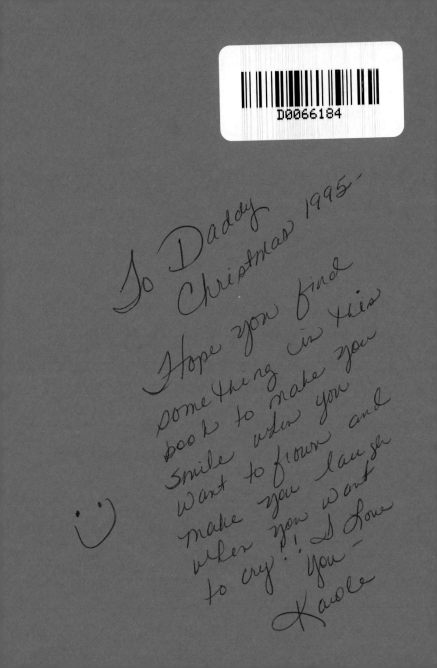

To Daddy
Christmas 1995 -

Hope you find
something in this
book to make you
smile when you
want to frown and
make you laugh
when you want
to cry!! I Love
You -
Karole

:)

THE
WIT AND WISDOM
of
Lewis Grizzard

Life Is Like A Dogsled Team...
If you're not the lead dog, the scenery never changes.

The
WIT AND WISDOM
of
Lewis Grizzard

Illustrations by
David Boyd

LONGSTREET PRESS
Atlanta, Georgia

Published by LONGSTREET PRESS, INC.,
a subsidiary of Cox Newspapers,
a division of Cox Enterprises, Inc.
2140 Newmarket Parkway
Suite 118
Marietta, Georgia 30067

Printed in the United States of America

1st printing, 1993

Library of Congress Catalog Number 94-74231

ISBN: 1-56352-215-2

This book was printed by Maple-Vail Book Group

Cover/jacket design by Jill Dible
Book design by Neil Hollingsworth

Grateful acknowledgment is made to Villard Books, a division of Random House, Inc., for permission to reprint an
exerpt from *My Daddy Was A Pistol and I'm A Son of A
Gun* © 1986.

The
Wit and Wisdom
of

Lewis Grizzard

For Jim Minter and Ludlow Porch; they fueled his fire.

the editor

INTRODUCTION

Excerpted from *My Daddy Was a Pistol and I'm a Son of a Gun* by Lewis Grizzard

People often ask me where I got the ability to be funny. That's easy. I got it from my daddy's side of the family. I got it from Daddy. Even at a very young age, I could tell the difference between my father's family and my mother's....

My maternal grandparents raised me and I loved them with all my heart. But they were quiet and spent a lot of time sitting under trees discussing the weather and who died recently. They were hard-working people, deeply religious, who warned me of the hellfire and of my streak of laziness that kept me from any interest in things I didn't enjoy doing, such as working in the fields where one tended to get very hot and dirty.

My mother's side of the family hated alcohol with a fierce passion. The Grizzards, however, would take a drink and they would sing and they would dance and they would tell funny stories. My daddy, even when his times were hardest, was never without a joke to tell some stranger he'd met thirty seconds earlier. I admit I am still stealing his material, still using characters that he forged first.

INTRODUCTION

There was Lucille Wellmaker, a stout girl with whom my father went to school. She wore "bermuda-alls," overalls cut off at the knee, and carried a wagon spoke to dances. If anybody refused to dance with her, in my daddy's words, she would "turn the whole place out with that wagon spoke."

There was Hester Camp, who was uglier than any empty glass of buttermilk, and there was Ollie Groves, who used to ride a pig to school.

And there were his jokes. God, I still remember them and when I tell them again, often I fall into my father's voice. I do a magnificent impression of my father's voice:

There was this ol' boy who up and died, and he had loved to eat cheese all his life. His wife decided she'd put a big piece of lemburger cheese in the casket with him.

These two friends of his were looking down at the ol' boy in the casket and they didn't know about the cheese. One of 'em up and said, "Lord, Lord, he looks like he could just up and talk."

The other, gettin' a whiff of that two-day-old cheese, said, "If he did what I think he just did, he'd better say, 'Excuse me....'"

Then there were these two preachers. There was this small town with a Baptist and a Methodist church. Both congregations had young preachers and they both rode bicycles to the services every Sunday morning, and every Sunday morning they would meet and exchange notes.

One morning, the Baptist preacher walked up on foot. The Methodist preacher said, "Brother, where is your bicycle?"

The Baptist preacher said, "Brother, I believe somebody in my congregation has stolen my bicycle."

The Methodist minister was appalled. He said, "I'll tell you how to get your bicycle back. You preach on the Ten Commandments this morning, and when you get to 'Thou shalt not steal,' you bear down on it. You make 'em feel that fire, smell that brimstone! Whoever stole your bicycle will start feeling bad and bring it back to you."

The Baptist preacher said he'd try it. The next Sunday morning, sure enough, he was on his bicycle again.

"Hallelujah!" shouted the Methodist preacher. "I see you preached on the Ten Commandments and got your bicycle back. I'll bet you had the thief really squirming when you bore down on 'Thou shalt not steal.'"

"Well, that's not exactly what happened," said the Baptist minister.

"What do you mean?" asked the Methodist preacher.

"Well, I did preach on the Ten Commandments," his colleague said, "but when I got to 'Thou shalt not commit adultery,' I remembered where I left my bicycle."

INTRODUCTION

He was a great people-watcher, my daddy. He saw funny where no one else would. He laughed at skinny, "wormy" men he'd see on the streets. Because the Grizzards were a rather large-in-the-waist group, whenever he'd see a fat woman he would say, "I believe that's one of the Grizzard girls."

He never met a waitress he didn't call "Pearl." Whenever he walked into a place to make a purchase and was not immediately waited on, he would offer up, in a loud, high-pitched voice, "I'm leav-*ing*." He once walked into a restaurant ... and noticed a sign that said, "All the fried chicken you can eat, $3.95."

He called the waitress over. "Pearl," he said, "is the management of this establishment prepared to back up this claim of all the fried chicken I can eat for $3.95?"

She said that it was.

"Then, dear woman," he said, "please alert the management that they are about to be in serious financial trouble."

That man could eat. God, how he could eat.... He loved fried chicken. He also loved country ham and homemade biscuits and he used to buy those sausages he called "red-hots," which he would fry for a late snack. He ate what he called a "Snellville milkshake" — cornbread soaking in a glass of buttermilk. One thing that was not passed down from my father to me was his affinity for buttermilk.

INTRODUCTION

But I do have his voice. I also got his love for a funny story. And his love for great characters, great one-liners. I got his love of being the center of attention and with that, the ability and material to have them rolling in the aisles....

Whatever talent I have, Daddy was the foundation of it.

— August 1986

THE
WIT AND WISDOM
of
Lewis Grizzard

I stopped eating boneless chicken dishes after I saw the farm in Maryland where they raise them. It'll break your heart to see those little boneless chickens try to walk.

The Wit and Wisdom of Lewis Grizzard

Bad luck is meeting your date's father and realizing he's the pharmacist you bought condoms from that afternoon.

∽

If love were oil, I'd be about a quart low.

∽

I really don't mind flying. It's the crashing and burning that bothers me.

∽

Why do fancy restaurants always cook the tomatoes and leave the green beans raw?

———◁◦▷———

Most of what I know about sex I learned hanging around the gas station as a kid. The first couple of times I heard anyone ask, "Gettin' any?" I thought they were talking about fish. When I finally figured it out, the responses made a lot more sense.

"Naw, not much," one fellow would reply. "My wife done cut me down to twice a week. But I guess I ought to count my blessings. She cut two other fellows clean out."

"Well, then are you gettin' any on the side?"

"Hell, I didn't even know they'd moved it!"

———◁◦▷———

3

The Wit and Wisdom of Lewis Grizzard

I have three ex-wives. I can't remember any of their names, so I just call 'em all Plaintiff.

ↄ৲০

Women who drink white wine either want to get married, sell you a piece of real estate, or redecorate your house. Either way, it's expensive.

ↄ৲০

If doctors make so much money, why can't they afford new magazines for their waiting rooms?

ↄ৲০

I don't hate Yankees, but I have a friend who does. His hobby is reading the obituary page of the *New York Times*.

Is it really necessary for bowling balls to weigh that much? Couldn't they just make the pins lighter?

There's a big difference between the words "naked" and "nekkid." Naked means you don't have any clothes on. "Nekkid" means you don't have any clothes on and you're up to something.

꙳

Chili dawgs always bark at night.

꙳

Most women who suffer from PMS also seem to have ESP. They're bitches who know everything.

꙳

I called my doctor one day and told him I had a bad case of diarrhea. He immediately put me on hold.

A man was standing on a street corner with a dog beside him. Another fellow walked up, smiled at the dog, and asked, "Does your dog bite?"

When the man answered, "No," the fellow bent down to pet the dog. Seconds later he pulled back a bloody, gnarled hand.

"I thought you said your dog didn't bite!" he yelled.

"He doesn't," said the first man. "But that's not my dog."

One girl in my high school class was late developing. Weyman C. Wannamaker, a great American, used to go up to her and say, "Laura Jane, I've got a joke that'll make you laugh your boobs off.... Oh, I see you've already heard it."

๑๖

One of my friends found a condom on the verandah. When he questioned his teen-aged son about it, the kid replied, "What's a verandah?"

๑๖

I never liked baths. Why would anyone want to wash their face in the same water they've been sitting in?

Why would anyone eat a mushroom? Don't they know that frogs go to the bathroom on those things?

Every time I think I know all the answers to modern-day questions, somebody changes the questions.

∽

I have it on good authority that Yankee men are so lazy they marry pregnant women.

∽

Judging from television commercials, there's a hemorrhoid epidemic in this country.

∽

There are only three ways to sleep on a train: be dead tired, dead drunk, or just plain dead.

A motorist traveling through Alabama stops for gas in a small town. As his tank is being filled, he looks across the street and notices the First Church of the Enlightened on one corner and the Second Church of the Enlightened on the opposite corner. Confused, he asks the attendant, "What's the difference in those two churches?"

"Very simple," the man answers. "The First Church of the Enlightened believes that Moses's mother found him in the bullrushes. The Second Church of the Enlightened believes, 'Yeah, that's what *she* says.'"

∽

When a dentist says, "This may sting a little," he really means, "How high can you jump?"

∾

Before I went on a cruise, I went to the drugstore and bought some condoms and motion-sickness pills. The smart-aleck pharmacist suggested that if it makes me sick, I should just get rid of my water bed.

∾

In the first twenty years of a man's life, his mother is always wondering where he's going. In the next twenty years, his wife wonders where he's been. Finally, when he dies, his friends wonder where he's at.

I was at a Georgia football game with a friend when Uga, the team's English Bulldog mascot, stopped at midfield and began licking his genitals. My friend said, "I wish I could do that." And I said, "That dog'll bite youuuuu!"

Golf is a lot like sex. You don't have to be very good at either one to enjoy it.

∞

For years I thought Oral Roberts University was a school of dentistry.

∞

Ever since I had a pig valve put in my heart, every afternoon about three I have this incredible urge to make love in the mud. Do you know how hard it is to find a woman with that same urge?

∞

Don't bend over in the garden, Granny; you know them taters got eyes.

I know this fellow who hangs out at the race track a lot. One evening after he went to sleep, his wife was cleaning out the pockets of his pants before sending them to the cleaners. She found a scrap of paper with the name Gladys and a phone number.

The next morning she confronted her husband. "Who is Gladys?" she demanded. "And how do you explain this phone number?"

"Gladys is a filly I bet on at the track yesterday, and the phone number is my bookie's," he said.

The next afternoon the fellow arrived home from the track and asked his wife, "Did I get any mail today?"

"No," she said, "but your horse called twice."

The *W*it and *W*isdom of *L*ewis *G*rizzard

———⌒⌒———

Why is it necessary to stand in line to deal with any branch of the government?

⌒⌒

In the summertime, I put ice tea in my thermos bottle and it stays cold. In the wintertime, I put hot coffee in my thermos and it stays hot. How do it know?

⌒⌒

I don't care if Michael Jackson turns out to be a boy or a girl. I just think he ought to be one or the other.

⌒⌒

A doctor friend of mine has a failproof way to prevent the spread of AIDS through sex — sit down and keep your mouth shut.

When I screamed at my dog for going to the bathroom on my carpet, he pointed out that I go to the bathroom in his water bowl.

17

One time I went to a small country church where the preacher was imploring his congregation to "tell it all," to confess their sins aloud. After an assortment of the usual sins, one ol' boy confessed to having had sex with his goat. The preacher said, "Damn, brother, I don't believe I'datold *that*!"

෨

If God had intended for man to fly, He wouldn't have given him the rental car and unlimited mileage.

෨

When my love returns from the ladies room, will I be too old to care?

The Wit and Wisdom of Lewis Grizzard

My conscience hasn't always been the best
judge of what's sinful and what's not, so I
came up with a sure-fire test. I just ask myself
three questions:

1. Is is fun?
2. Does it feel good?
3. Is it fattening?

If the answer to any of those questions
is *Yes*, you can bet your MYF pin that it's a sin.

Why is it that those slick TV evangelists who want you to give money for the Lord's work always give you their address?

ᘓᘏ

Is it really necessary to print "USE ONLY AS DIRECTED" on a tube of hemorrhoid medicine?

ᘓᘏ

Sex just hasn't been the same since women started enjoying it.

ᘓᘏ

Shoot low, boys! They're ridin' Shetland ponies!

Why is it that a woman will scratch a dog's belly but won't scratch her man's?

A man came in from a long afternoon of golf. His wife met him at the door with a kiss. A few minutes later their son came in looking tired and weary.

"Where's he been?" asked the father.

"He's been caddying for you all afternoon," said his wife.

"No wonder that kid looked so familiar."

∾

I'm always hearing about consenting adults, but personally I have the hardest time getting female adults to consent. "Let's just be friends," is the line I hear most often. If I wanted a friend, I'd visit Mr. Rogers' neighborhood.

⸺◀o▶⸺

A good many years ago, before the widespread use of ultrasound to determine an unborn child's sex, three pregnant women were sitting in their doctor's waiting room.

"I'm going to have a boy," said one of the women.

"How do you know that?" asked another.

"Everybody knows that when the man is on top during conception, you'll have a boy."

"Oh," said the first woman. "I guess that means I'll be having a girl, because I was on top during our conception."

The third woman in the room burst into tears.

"What's wrong, honey?" asked the first woman.

Between sobs, the third woman said, "I'm going to have puppies."

⸺◀o▶⸺

Relative humidity? That's how much you sweat when you're making love to your cousin.

❦

Ours is the only country in the world where people pay $200,000 for a house and then leave it for two weeks every summer to sleep in a tent.

❦

You know why Junior Leaguers hate group sex? All those thank-you notes.

❦

The only difference between *Playboy* and *National Geographic* is that Hugh Hefner took the baskets off the women's heads.

My ex-wives had one thing in common: When they left, they all backed up a truck.

At Clemson University, a major Southern agricultural school, they've discovered a new use for sheep — wool.

∞

I saw an ad the other day for a fine leather pouch that holds condoms. I guess that's for the man who has everything but doesn't want to catch anything.

∞

There's something wrong when you wait in line for thirty minutes to get a hamburger that was cooked for ninety seconds an hour ago.

Two old men in their eighties had been playing golf together for years. One day during a round they were pondering "golf after life."

"Do you think there's golf in heaven?" said the first.

"I sure hope so," said the second. "I tell you what. Let's make a pact. Whoever dies first will come back and tell the other."

Sure enough, about three weeks later the first fellow died. Shortly thereafter, as his friend lay in bed, he heard a voice.

"Bill? Bill? Is that you?"

"Yes, it's me. And I've come back to tell you about heaven."

"So, is there golf there?"

"Well, there's good news and bad. The good news is that yes, there's golf in heaven. All the fairways are lush and wide, all the greens are large and smooth, and everybody shoots par."

"So what's the bad news?"

"The bad news is that you've got a tee time next Tuesday."

Jimmy Swaggart and Jerry Falwell were on a flight together. The stewardess asked Swaggart if he would like a drink, and he ordered Scotch. Then she turned to Falwell for his order. In a firm voice he said, "I'd rather commit adultery than partake of alcohol."

Swaggart said, "Me too, but I didn't know we had a choice!"

∽

If I ran my affairs like the government, I'd be like a homeless snake — I wouldn't have a pit to hiss in.

∽

I saw a sign on a church marquee recently that said, "Tired of Sin? Come on in!" Underneath someone had scrawled, "If not, call Shirley, 555-3132."

I'm not against women's libertation. I've given three their freedom myself.

Baptists never make love standing up. They're afraid someone might see them and think they're dancing.

∽

Why do service stations lock the bathroom door but leave the cash register unlocked?

∽

My grandmother always believed that the moon shot was fake but rasslin' was real.

∽

When you live alone, the phone is always for you.

To me, there's only one kind of snake — the dreaded copperheaded water rattler. If you run from it, it'll chase you. If you lock yourself inside your house and hide in a closet, it'll wait outside until you finally come out for food. And if you happen to sneak past it at home, it knows where you work. Now tell me about good snakes.... Ain't no such thing.

———∽———

Do you know the difference between a Rolls Royce and a porcupine?

With a porcupine, the prick is on the outside.

∽

There's an old story about two fellows watching an unattractive woman cross the street.

"Lordy, that Cordie Mae Poovey is uglier than a train wreck," says one.

"Don't be so rough on her," says the other. "She can't help being ugly."

"Maybe not," says the first, "but she could have at least stayed home!"

∽

I believe we should get sex out of the pulpit and back into politics where it belongs.

There is only one excuse needed for anything that doesn't work in this country: The computer is down.

I hated shopping for antiques when I was married. But I have to admit, it beats shopping for antiques in a bar at closing time.

൭

Never marry a woman who has an extensive knowledge of nautical terms and can tie over 200 knots.

൭

Real estate agents are God's curse on mankind when locusts are out of season.

൭

I'm bad to get into what Southerners describe as "sorry spells" — too sorry to work and too sorry to care if I don't.

34

This attractive young lady said she'd like to go out with me but was worried about my being a lot older. I told her, "Listen, guys like me, we're like used cars. Sure, we've been around the block a time or two, but a good one is cheaper and more dependable than a new car. And the older we get, the cuddlier we get."

"I see your point," the young lady said, "but I don't think I'd like to be married to a used car."

"Why not?" I asked.

She said, "Did you ever try to crank one of those things on a cold morning?"

ক৹

Why doesn't the Surgeon General do something about Mexican TV dinners? Every year they kill countless thousands of single men.

ক৹

In a romantic moment I once asked my wife, "Darling, do we have mutual orgasms?" She cooly answered that we were insured by Prudential.

ক৹

I'm still not sure what sodomy is, but I know for a fact that all my ex-wives were against it.

ক৹

By the time a man can afford to lose a golf ball, he can't hit it that far.

Never marry a woman who carries a coin changer on her belt.

Automobiles — and everything else mechanical — confuse me. For years I thought a McPherson strut was one of those dances I couldn't do in the seventies.

✺

A university professor recently received a grant to study why the oppossum crossed the road. Well, actually it was to study why so many possums are killed while crossing roads. I can save him a lot of time: they're suicidal. They jump in front of cars because they're the ugliest animals on earth. I can also tell him why they're called O-possums: because just before a car runs them over, they say, "O hell, I'm a goner now!"

---◆◇◆---

An evangelist was praying to God one time and said, "God, what's a million dollars to you?"

And God answered, "A penny."

So the evangelist said, "God, what's a million years to you?"

And God said, "A second."

So the evangelist said, "Well then, God, wouldn't you please just lend a penny to this poor servant?"

And God said, "Just a second."

---◆◇◆---

A rotund golfer was arguing for more shots when the bet was being made. "You guys have a tremendous advantage over me because I have to putt from memory."

"From memory? What are you talking about?" asked his opponent.

"Well," he said, patting his ample belly, "when I put the ball where I can see it, I can't reach it; and when I put it where I can reach it, I can't see it."

The only good thing that ever came out of Chicago was I-65 South.

I've often wondered if Yasir Arafat has a brother somewhere named Nossir.

Women must be the only sex with ESP, because they always know if men are going to get laid.

∞

How can I trust a bank to keep my money safe when it has dozens of pens stolen every day?

∞

Getting other people to do your work is the cornerstone of free enterprise.

∞

Every time I hear about a quarterback finding the Lord, I wonder if he'll finally be able to find his secondary receivers.

I used to fish a lot because I thought it was relaxing, but it got to be too much trouble. Then a friend told me his theory: "If you truly fish for relaxation, don't bait your hook. Now, that's relaxing!"

This same friend, a Southerner suspicious of anything Northern (he won't even eat Great Northern Beans), also told me, "The only way to make ice hockey interesting is to paint the puck white."

If you spit on the subway in New York, they'll fine you $25. But you can throw up for nothing.

෧෨

The greatest form of birth control known to man is a Bronx accent.

෧෨

Instead of having your face lifted, why not have your body lowered?

෧෨

The best thing about living alone is that whenever you find a hair in your soup, you always know whose it is.

Never eat barbecue in a place that also sells Dover sole.

Ten million people live in New York City, where the air is foul, the streets are dirty, and crime is rampant. Hardly anybody lives in Yellville, Arkansas, where the mountain air is refreshing, there are clear streams and rivers for fishing and boating, and you don't have to lock you doors at night. WHY?

ᖆ

Bachelors never have to hear, "Honey, there's something important I've been meaning to talk to you about," when Dallas is fourth-and-one on Washington's two-yard line.

ᖆ

The best scam I ever heard of was the service station owner who put a condom machine in the ladies bathroom but didn't put any condoms in it. He said no one ever complained.

———————◁○▷———————

There are so few trees in parts of West Texas that small boys have to take a number and wait to climb one. When I asked a friend what it was like to live in such a place, she said, "The best way I can describe it is this way: A prisoner broke out of the county jail and three days later the newspaper called to see if the escapee had been captured. The sheriff said, 'What's the hurry? I can still see him running.'"

———————◁○▷———————

When a politician says, "We've run a clean, honest campaign," he really means, "I spent $30,000 on private detectives and those peckerwoods didn't find a speck of dirt on my opponent."

A Northern Baptist preacher will tell you, "There ain't no hell." A Southern Baptist preacher will tell you, "The hell there ain't!"

When you ask a pouting woman, "What's wrong?" and she answers, "Nothing," there's something seriously wrong... and it's all your fault.

Chicago has two seasons — winter and the Fourth of July.

Kinky is when you use duck feathers in making love. Perverted is when you use the *whole* duck.

∾

Contrary to what New York City taxi drivers may think, oral sex does not mean shouting sexual insults at the guy in front of you.

∾

Why doesn't someone take Mohammar Khadafy hostage and demand that he get all his people out of our convenience stores?

∾

One TV commercial proclaims, "These feminine napkins are disposable." Why on earth would anybody want to keep one?

People sometimes make fun of the University of Georgia, where I graduated. They say if you drive through Athens real slow with your window rolled down, they'll throw a diploma in your car. But I'm here to tell you that's a lie.... You have to stop.

Never go on a camping trip with a man who drinks whiskey sours.

෧෨

The three most overrated things in the world are extramarital sex, fancy restaurants, and Rock City.

෧෨

Did you hear about the preacher who took all the church's money and went to Las Vegas? Part of the money he gambled away. Part of it he spent on booze. Part of it he spent on wild woman. And the rest he just squandered.

I have noticed that my body is taking on a more rounded shape toward the middle. I understand it's caused by fallen chest arches.

I never knew exactly what a "line shack" was, but there was one in every western movie, and nothing good ever happened there.

Gin drinkers are the types who leave the house to get a loaf of bread, drop by the bar for "just one," and return home six weeks later...with the bread.

The toughest thing in the world is *not* walking across the dance floor to ask a young woman to dance. The toughest thing is the long walk back after she says no.

---◄◊►---

One day a priest was playing golf on the fabled Muirfield course in Scotland. He hit a tee shot into a deep fairway bunker and found his ball buried in sand at the base of a bunker wall four-feet high. The priest looked at his ball, turned his face to Heaven and said, "God, help me." Then he looked back at the ball, turned again toward Heaven and added, "And, God, don't send Jesus. This is no shot for a boy!"

---◄◊►---

The only time I ever got lucky playing blackjack in Vegas was the night I got sleepy and went to bed.

Who was the first person to eat an oyster?

Why does every dentist in America fill your mouth with cotton and *then* ask who'll win tomorrow's game?

Any woman who doesn't know how World War II turned out is too young to date.

I wish Queen Elizabeth would give the Cisco Kid his hat back.

You know you're getting old when you stop buying green bananas.

ை

If the President gets hemorrhoids and is treated by a Naval physician, does he have to be a rear admiral?

ை

You know kids are having sex too early in life when your daughter buys a box of Cracker Jacks and the prize is a diaphragm.

ை

If you live in the Northeast and don't attend Sunday School regularly, when you die you go to Newark.

My mother always wanted me to be a preacher. She said, "Son, as good a speaker as you are, you could make a million dollars as a preacher."

"But, Mama," I always answered, "what the hell would I spend it on?"

Why do we have to call the places airplanes fly into and out of "terminals"?

∞

If gay men can go in the men's bathrooms, why can't heterosexual men go in the women's bathrooms?

∞

Where does fat go when you lose it?

∞

The world around me is a tuxedo, and I'm a pair of brown shoes.

Is there some sort of FAA regulation that requires a crying baby to travel on every flight?

The Wit and Wisdom of Lewis Grizzard

One of the things that's wrong with our society today is that most folks are too pretentious to hang their underwear out to dry on a clothesline so any passerby can see.

∿

If fish are supposed to have scales, why do anchovies have hair?

∿

I know lots of people who are educated far beyond their intelligence.

∿

Beauty may be only skin deep, but ugly goes clear to the bone.

The golf pro is giving a lesson to one of his club members. "Now, first of all, just take a few swings without hitting the ball," says the pro.

"Hell, I've already mastered that shot," says the member. "I'm paying you to teach me how to *hit* it."

Why is it that when you ask a woman if she wants some popcorn, she always says, "No, I'll just have a bite of yours"?

∽

Don't let your mouth write a check your ass can't cash.

∽

Dale Evans is largely to blame for the women's movement. She kept her maiden name and never rode sidesaddle.

∽

If gooses is geese, then how come mooses ain't meese?

The next time I feel the urge to get married, I think
I'll just find a woman I hate and buy her a house.

A lot of men put cellular phones in their cars to impress women. In the old days, we hung foam rubber dice from the rear-view mirror for the same reason.

‹∿›

My biggest worry about the future is learning to count in yen.

‹∿›

The best thing about owning a basset hound is that no matter how bad you feel, the basset always looks worse.

‹∿›

Why are women allowed to sell men's under-wear?

The Wit and Wisdom of Lewis Grizzard

When women see the two-minute warning in a football game, they think that means it'll be only two minutes until the game is over. Fifteen minutes later, when there's still thirty seconds left on the clock, they look totally confused. "It's very simple," I explained to my wife. "It's just like when we're late for a dinner reservation and you say, 'I'll be ready in two minutes.'"

I always thought Janis Joplin was Missouri's entry in the Miss America pageant.

ↄ∿ↄ

The main problem in the world today boils down to the fact that the opposite sex isn't nearly as opposite as it used to be.

ↄ∿ↄ

Why does a major league second baseman who can't hit his weight make more money than the President of the United States?

ↄ∿ↄ

Never send back food in a restaurant where the cook is wearing a sidearm.

The thing that would help televised golf tournaments most is for the PGA to require the players to spit and scratch their privates.

———∽———

I'm not saying Kim Basinger is gorgeous, but I'd marry her dog just to be part of the family.

∽

I don't care what anyone says — I know for a fact that the more sympathy you get when you're sick, the faster you recover.

∽

It's better to have died a small child than to be a politician who gets caught in a scandal during a slow news month.

∽

Bucket seats have done more to separate the sexes than the Southern Baptist Convention.

I was standing at a urinal beside two fellows at a Georgia-Auburn football game. The Georgia fan finished his business, zipped his pants, and headed for the door. "Hey, Bulldog," shouted the Auburn fan, "don't they teach you guys to wash your hands after using the bathroom?" The Georgia fan replied, "No, they teach us not to pee on our hands."

Putting grits on ant beds is an old remedy for getting rid of them. Serving unbuttered, unsalted instant grits has the same effect on Yankee tourists.

৩

Our parents' sex lives were much simpler. All they had to do was memorize one position and remember to turn off the lights.

৩

Reading *Playboy* magazine is my alternative to jogging. I look at the pictures until my heart rate reaches 190, then I put it down.

The only way to make hunting a sport is to give the animals guns so they can shoot back.

Yankees sometimes make fun of the South, but I've never once seen anyone in an Atlanta bar celebrating because they were being transferred to New Jersey.

⌘

Has anyone ever put out an eye because they were running with a sharp stick in their hand? My mother warned me about that every day of my childhood.

⌘

God bless Merle Haggard. He actually did all the things that Johnny Cash was supposed to have done.

⌘

If we educate today's athletes, how can we expect them to understand their coaches?

I saw a sign on the side of the road advertising deep fried pork skins. In keeping with today's healthy attitudes, the sign said, "Our pork skins cooked in 100% vegetable oil." Think about it a minute; it'll come to you.

It's a sad commentary on the state of higher education when the best a college student can come up with on the sidelines is, "Hi, Mom!"

෨෧

Remember when "going all the way" meant a trip to the state capital?

෨෧

I've always wondered what John Smith used for an alias when he checked into the Motel 6 with Pocahontas.

෨෧

How much does the Greyhound Bus company pay people to sit beside me and cough?

Some country clubs are so exclusive they won't allow you in until you've had your first heart surgery.

Pornography does, in fact, have an effect on men. I grew up thinking that all women had a staple in their navel.

❧

I was standing next to a fellow at a bar late one night. Shortly before midnight, he suddenly picked up a beer can and threw it across the room. "What the hell are you doing?" I asked. "Throwing it out of bounds, trying to stop the clock," he answered.

❧

Cordie Mae Poovey was so fat in high school that when the gym teacher told her to haul ass, she had to make two trips.

The Wit and Wisdom of Lewis Grizzard

---◦◦◦---

---◦◦---

I believe that all country music should fall under one of the following categories:

Cheatin' Songs: She ran off.
Forgivin' Songs: She came back.
Hurtin' Songs: The hussy ran off again.
Drinkin' Songs: Nobody here to cook, so I might as well get drunk.
Train Songs: She ran off on a train; I think I'll derail that sucker.
Prison Songs: They take derailing trains seriously.
Rodeo Songs: Soon as she got out of the hospital after the train wreck, she took up with a bullrider.
Never-Give-Up-Hope Songs: I wonder if her sister still lives in Tupelo.

---◦◦---

My grandfather didn't like it when preachers used note cards to deliver their sermons. "They ought to get it straight from the Lord," he said many a time. "Politicians use notes."

∽

Money doesn't grow on trees, and if it did, somebody else would own the orchard.

∽

Where did convenience stores get their name? They're not.

∽

What's so scary in women's bathrooms that no woman ever wants to go alone?

When a politician says, "The people have spoken," what he really means is, "If I'd known I had this many enemies, I would have carried a gun."

The Wit and Wisdom of Lewis Grizzard

Time flies like an arrow; fruit flies like a banana.

∽

I have occasionally been praised for my book titles, but several of my better offerings were never used. Obviously a case of editors without taste:

- The Adventures of Johnny Condomseed
- Hold Her, Slim, She's Headin' for the Briar Patch
- Satanic Nurses
- Tammy Faye Baker is Uglier Than a Bowling Shoe
- Hung Up on Hangin' Out
- Fenced Yards and Hole Cards Can Ruin Your Outlook on Life

I guess it's true that pornography leads to crime. I saw a story in the newspaper yesterday about a man in Fargo, North Dakota, who read a copy of *Hustler* magazine one morning and was caught that afternoon trying to make an early withdrawal on his certificate of deposit at the bank. Another fellow who was watching the *Playboy* channel from bed was caught tearing the "Do not remove under penalty of law" tags off his mattress and pillows.

The first time I saw a live woman naked, I was surprised that she didn't have a basket of fruit on her head.

❧

The main source of inferiority complexes in America is the *Penthouse* Advisor. When was the last time you got the wrong shirts from the laundry and ended up having sex inside a dryer while her girlfriend stuffed quarters in the slot?

❧

Dr. Ruth's heavy accent worries me. A comment from her about group sex could lead to a run on grouper at the local fishmarket.

❧

The greatest gag of all time is the French tickler.

Although I've never caught them in the act, I know for a fact that beer cans breed in the back floor-board of your car.

Show me a man with a Rolls Royce and I'll show you a man who has had sex in the back seat.

∞

If the mechanic making last-minute checks underneath your airplane is named Bubba, I'd wait for the next flight.

∞

I was turned down for a security clearance last week. They said I once forgot to return my seat to its original locked and upright position before take-off. I'm sorry.

∞

I've been married three times, but many women auditioned for the part.

It's no wonder that most young boys grow up confused about authority. When I was a teen-ager at the county fair, the barker for the burlesque show would shout, "No one under 18 or over 80 allowed inside! If you're under 18, you wouldn't understand it; if you're over 80, you couldn't take it!" Then he would wink as he took the half-dollar from my hand. That night at the truck stop, when we ordered a beer, Shorty would point to the ratty sign on the wall that said, "B-21 or B-Gone." Then he'd say, "Can you read that? If you can, you gotta be over 21!"

When I was twelve, baseball was my life. When I was fourteen, I saw Kathy Sue Loudermilk in a tight sweater, and baseball didn't seem nearly as important. Now that I'm over forty, every time I see a woman in a tight sweater all I can think about is the feel of that baseball in my hand.

I once dropped a dollop of Preparation H on one shoe. By the next morning I had one size 9 and one size 5.

A woman editor at a northern newspaper recently dropped my column. She said I was sexist. The dumb broad probably doesn't even shave her legs.

The Environmental Protection Agency recently presented me an award … for recycling my jokes.

I know why Mohammar Khadafy is so mean. His mama didn't like him. Otherwise, she wouldn't have named him Mohammar.

Who are they kidding on airplanes when they say, "In the unlikely event that there is a loss of cabin pressure, reach out, place the oxygen mask over your nose and face, and breathe normally"?

In the unlikely event of a loss of cabin pressure on my plane, I'm going to breathe like Secretariat down the stretch.

∽

Be prepared to lose even your most valued personal possessions in a divorce. I've lost, among other things, several sofas and beds, one good dog, a number of television sets, and my priceless Faron Young albums. She didn't even like Faron Young, but she told a friend she enjoyed watching the records melt in the fire.

The greatest name I ever gave a dog was Dudley Upshaw Macbeth Beasley, American Skunk Sniffer. Here's how I came up with that name:

- Dudley was my best friend.
- Upshaw was for a slack-armed major league pitcher, Cecil Upshaw, who was my role model at the time.
- Macbeth was the play my English teacher kept harping about; the ghosts, sex and stabbings sounded great, but I could never make it past the first five pages.
- Beasley was for Janette Beasley, who was two years ahead of me in school and whose under wear I had seen hanging on the clothesline behind her house.
- And American Skunk Sniffer is self-explanatory.

We bathed him in everything from Tide to turpentine and still couldn't kill the stink. That's when I came up with his nickname, from the first letters of his full name: D-U-M-B-A-S-S. It described him perfectly.

I'm no match for a crying woman. I'll promise her anything from a car to dinner with her mama if she'll just stop. One crying woman almost got me to vote for Michael Dukakis. I promised I would, but then at the last minute I remembered the secret ballot.

∽

I was a pitcher for my high school baseball team. I had pretty good "junk," but my coach was not impressed by my speed: "Damn, Lewis, you're not even bruising their bats. They're hitting you like a nag down the stretch."

∽

I wish my grandfather had lived long enough to see folks pay $2 for a bottle of water.

∽

"The Arabs are trying to buy America," one of my friends complained. "Don't worry," I said. "The Japanese won't sell it to them."

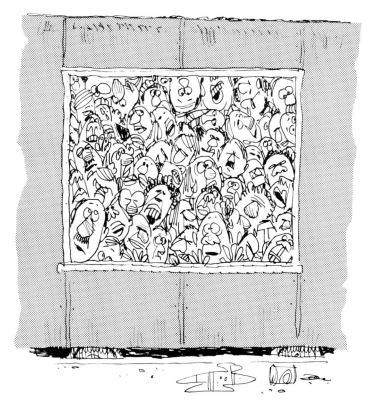

No matter how crowded a subway car looks, it can always hold one more.

I used to tell my fans that all the proceeds from sales of my books went to my little brother Joey, so he could have his operation. Well, thanks to you all, Joey finally had the operation. He's now Joanne; he works as a cocktail waitress and plays golf from the ladies' tees.

෮෯

A hunter friend of mine says, "If we don't kill off part of the deer population every year, they'll starve to death." Why don't they just take them some food?

෮෯

Why do women think that a closet without 416 pair of shoes is like a necklace with no earrings to match?

I have broken a lot of hard-hitting news stories over the years on such things as salad bars (they always put those little tomatoes way in the back so you can't reach them); buttermilk (it comes from cows who eat dirt); Mohammar Khadafy (who is really the same person as baseball pitcher Joacquin Andujar); seat cushions on airplanes (they really can't be used as flotation devices); and buttered popcorn (it's really flavored with buttermilk).

What do you call an Iraqi with an IQ of 120?
A village.

∽

My favorite song title: "I Can't Get Over You Until You Get Out From Under Him."

∽

What's so special about "free-range chicken"? When I was growing up, everybody in my family had "free-yard chickens."

∽

My boyhood friend and idol, Weyman C. Wannamaker, Jr., was once asked, "Are you a member of the Klan? That's the rumor going 'round." Weyman said, "No, you just misunderstood. What they said is I'm a booger under the sheets."

You know how they start the baseball season in Chicago? The mayor thaws out the first ball.

Weyman C. Wannamaker, Jr., a great American, once paid Kathy Sue Loudermilk the highest compliment I have ever heard: "I've been to three county fairs, two square dances, and a Shriner parade. I've seen a chicken play the piano, a baboon that knew his ABCs, and a duck fart under water. But," he went on, nodding toward Kathy Sue, "I ain't never seen a dog that'll hunt like that."

∞

Southerners didn't fight in the Civil War to save slavery. They were fighting to make Yankee men dress better when they visited Southern beaches. They desperately wanted Yankee men to stop wearing black socks with their sandals and Bermuda shorts. Unfortunately they lost...which is why so many Yankee men dress like that on Southern beaches today. To the victor go the spoils.

The Wit and Wisdom of Lewis Grizzard

Miss Inez Puckett had been bothered by bad kidneys all her life, despite the best efforts of doctors, chiropractors, and root witches. So one night, when Brother Roy Dodd's tent revival was in town, she staggered up on stage to try faith healing. Brother Roy laid hands on her, broke out in tongues, and then said, "You're healed! Praise the Lord!" Miss Inez felt the Spirit inside her and began jumping around the stage in celebration. She became so excited, however, that she fell off the stage and broke her leg. Several men from the audience rushed to her aid. One suggested that an ambulance be called. Another said, "We don't need no ambulance. Just get Brother Roy Dodd to heal her leg like he healed her kidneys." Brother Roy stepped back and said, "I think you'd better call the ambulance. I don't do broken bones, just internal organs."

I was on a nonstop flight from Atlanta to Los Angeles. The fellow sitting next to me said, "Going to Los Angeles?" I said, "I hope so. I really hope so."

❧

I never eat on airplanes. That way I never have to loosen my grip.

❧

I try not to think any dirty thoughts on an airplane so that God will like me and listen to my prayers.

❧

Has any man in America ever bought a brass duck? Has any woman in America ever NOT bought a brass duck?

If gays can't reproduce, how come there're so many more now than there used to be?

Why is it that the biggest, softest towels in the house are always in the guest bathroom, while I'm left to dry off with thread-bare hotel leftovers? And why can't I use the little soap in the shape of a rose?

❦

As far as I'm concerned, chickens have only two purposes in this world — to lay eggs and to be fried. I'm not interested in anything else you can do with a chicken.

❦

Why do women love "ini" foods so much? Zucchini, fettuccini, Tetrazzini…. One night my wife served hot dogs with noodles over them. When I complained, she said, "It's just Italian-style hot dogs." Oh no, I thought to myself: Weenieini.

According to my mother, who was most discreet about the whole thing, I was conceived on a train somewhere south of Atlanta. My father, on leave from the Army, was impatient. Not long after this revelation, I was in a bar when a young lady asked me what sign I was born under. "Well," I said, "if you consider the moment of conception as the actual date of first life, I may have been born under a sign that read DINING CAR IN OPPOSITE DIRECTION."

People have been telling me for years that I'm safer in an airplane than in an automobile, but I don't buy that. If a car develops a problem, you just pull off the road and park it. Try pulling an airplane into the emergency lane when the engines go out.

∽

A recently divorced friend of mine used the classified ads to get dates — not the Personals section, but the Automotive section. He advertised himself as a "clean one-owner."

∽

I came home from work one day and found my wife in tears. She said her four-year-old son (my stepson) had run away. "Don't cry," I said, "he'll come back." She looked up through teary eyes and said, "He already did. Why do you think I'm crying?"

In the words of my late father, who fought the Germans, the Chinese and the North Koreans, "Son, there's nothing meaner than a quarrelsome woman."

The Wit and Wisdom of Lewis Grizzard

The next time you're in a store shopping with your wife, notice that there are no clocks or windows in the women's department. Merchants, like casino operators, don't want their customers deterred by such trivial considerations as time.

ᏜᏜ

Do you know why Mike Tyson always cries when he makes love? Mace.

ᏜᏜ

One reason women need more clothes than men is that women's clothes age faster than men's. After a garment has hung in a woman's closet for more than two weeks, it is referred to as "that old thing."

ᏜᏜ

After missing a short putt on the golf course one day, I uttered a small oath (just enough to express my disappointment). One of my playing companions said, "You know, the best golfers don't use foul language." I snapped back, "I guess not. What the hell do they have to cuss about?"

---◄○►---

I asked a pilot friend of mine what advice he would offer to anyone in an "emergency situation." He said, "If anything happens to the plane or there are signs of trouble, I advise the following: Bend down as far as you can behind the seat in front of you. Grab each ankle securely. Place your head between your legs and...." I finished his sentence; I had heard it before. "I know, stay calm," I said. "No," he answered, "I was gonna say, just kiss your ass good-bye."

---◄○►---

I always follow the legendary advice of tennis great Ilie Nastase. When his American Express card was stolen in New York, reporters asked if he was trying to get it back. "No," said Nastase. "Whoever stole it is spending less than my wife was."

∞

A "sensitive man" is the one who orders white wine and a salad for lunch while all his buddies order a beer and a burger.

∞

After I got married, I learned the difference between "our money" and "my money." "Our money" was used to pay bills and buy food, gasoline and other necessities of life. "My money" was always spent on darling skirts and blouses.

I've come up with a way to get even with rude desk clerks at hotels: When you shower, don't put the curtain inside the tub.

Love is when you bring her a present and it's not a special occasion. Lust is when you bought it at Frederick's of Hollywood and Candy Barr wouldn't be caught dead wearing it.

ᕯᕯ

Love is when you met at a church social. Lust is when she answered your ad in *Hustler*.

ᕯᕯ

Love is when you take a romantic cruise together aboard a sailboat. Lust is when the boat belongs to your secretary's husband, who is in Cleveland on business.

ᕯᕯ

Love is when you invite her to a movie. Lust is when it's playing in your bedroom...the one with the mirrored ceiling.

Beware of beautiful young women with nice tans who are hungry when you meet them. They know the difference between French and domestic champagne. They'll wear the writing off your credit card.

I'm bad about leaving wadded up money in my pants pocket. One of my wives used to refer to doing the laundry as "Drying for Dollars."

〇〇

Why is it that in most newspapers the obituaries appear in the back of the "Living" section?

〇〇

A girlfriend of mine enjoyed the company of gay men, but suddenly she stopped going out with them. When I asked why, she said, "I got tired of going out with guys who were better looking than me."

There are seven places in the human body where nurses can stick a tube without making a new hole. I don't believe God ever intended for tubes to be stuck in several of those holes.

One lesson of growing older: Convertible sports cars attract giggly teen-aged girls, not women.

∽

I'm actually a serial killer. I can't tell you how many women, when I asked them out, said, "I'm sorry, but my grandmother just died, and I have to go to her funeral."

∽

Do you know what Bill Clinton always does when he finishes making love? Goes home.

The Wit and Wisdom of Lewis Grizzard

The most abusive (and also the best) golf caddies in the world are in Scotland. One once said to me, "You have a great short game, sir. Too bad it's off the tee." After duffing a shot, I said, "You know, golf's a funny game." To which my caddy replied, "It's not supposed to be, sir." Later I asked why he kept looking at his watch. He answered, "It's not a watch, sir; it's a compass." Finally, at the end of that round, I tried my hand at revenge: "You must be the worst caddy in the world," I said. And he answered, "That, sir, would be too great a coincidence."

I come from a large family. In fact, I never slept alone until I was married.